MANDALAS
For Fun and Relaxation

ADULT COLORING BOOK

Vanessa Bentley

Copyright © Vanessa Bentley 2017

All rights reserved. No part of this publication may be reproduced, distributed, or transmitted in any form or by any means, including photocopying, recording, or other electronic or mechanical methods, without the prior written, dated and signed permission of the copyright owner.

ISBN-13: 978-1978132047
ISBN-10: 1978132042

I have always found drawing to be a great way to relax and unwind. The simplicity or complexity of my drawings depends on my mood at the time. I hope that you will enjoy coloring them as much as I enjoyed drawing them.

There are no rules to coloring these designs, just enjoy them and have fun.

Vanessa

50 Original Mandalas for you to color. Some are really easy and some are complex enough to keep your mind off all your worries for a few hours.

A variety of materials can be used to color these images, from color pencils to markers. To prevent bleed-through when coloring, place a blank sheet of paper between the pages.

Images have been printed on one side of the page only.

All images in this book are original drawings and designs by Vanessa Bentley.

www.vanessabentley.com

You can use this page to test your art materials

www.ingramcontent.com/pod-product-compliance
Lightning Source LLC
Chambersburg PA
CBHW080852260726
48660CB00009B/3288